GW00367968

THE ONLY GOOD BANK MANAGER IS *HELEN*!

A Field Guide by
JOHN JENSEN

Happy Christmas

1991

SOUVENIR PRESS

The Banks represented in this book are fictitious
and bear no resemblance to any known Banks,
open or closed.
Any Banks finding similarities to themselves
should feel ashamed and apologise.

John Jensen

First published 1991 by Souvenir Press Ltd,
43 Great Russell Street, London WC1B 3PA
and simultaneously in Canada

ISBN 0 285 63071 7

Printed in Great Britain by
BPCC Hazells, Aylesbury
Photoset by Intype Ltd

'With this one you get interest on your current account and you have an agreed overdraft limit without penalties. But if you go over that limit we crack your balls.'

'Let me be the first to congratulate you.
Your Bank's crash has made the *Guinness
Book of Records*.'

'With the Compliments of the Manager.'

'By putting everything on computer and working through head office we can make great savings which we are, of course, able to pass on to our customers.'

'Shall I need to fill in a form? I want to withdraw my goodwill.'

'I'd better get the auditors in. He's the computer buff I put in charge of customers' accounts.'

'Next petitioner, please.'

'I used to be a financial wizard. I once made an entire banking empire disappear.'

'The sleeves have gone on all my jackets.
I always listen to my customers with my
head cupped in my hands.'

'Now that the Board of Directors has voted you a 115% salary increase, your current account is quite healthy.

'Unfortunately, I have orders to pull the rug from under your Company.'

'See! First it ate my card. Now it's toying with my emotions.'

'In view of Higginbotham's continued
absence in the South Seas, our
Treasurer's Report will be read in his
stead by Inspector Pemberthy of the
Serious Fraud Office.'

'If our computer *still* thinks it isn't time for you to have a new cheque book, perhaps we should ask ourselves *why* the computer still thinks it isn't time for you to have a new cheque book.'

'You misunderstand, Mr Pugh. This isn't
where you complain to *us*. This is where
we complain to *you*!'

'Mr Pilgrim is downstairs with his Chief
Accountant, his solicitor, a senior official
from the Department of Fair Trading, a
representative from the Ombudsman's
office, and journalists from *The Times*, *The
Financial Times* and *The Money Programme*.
Shall I tell them you're busy?'

'I admire your integrity, James, but head office would much rather you changed it back to "Advances".'

'Can I offer you refreshment?'

'Not too early for you, is it, Charles?'

'I know you're not allowed to launder money, but it's a pity you can't wash and iron your filthy old used fives.'

'Old Mayhew is spelling out the difference between a depositor's interest rate and a lender's interest rate.'

'*Awfully* sorry for inadvertently
clobbering you with double interest on
your overdraft, and for taking *such* a time
to rectify it . . .'

'Bank charges? You've come to the right branch, Mr Parkes. Our policy is to ask a mere 16% *maximum* overcharge.'

'Here's your temporary cheque book. Beg
nicely . . .'

'Frankly, you must be more than a student of life to qualify for a student account.'

'We've read all your letters to the Press
complaining about this Bank's
performance, Mrs Green, and
management has agreed that something
must be done, and quickly. So we're
closing your account.'

'And do we call our Bank charges
"Indirect Debits"?'

'I want you to think of me as a father. I'm going to cut you off without a penny.'

'I'd like to buy some cheap money.'

'To your right, please, Colonel. You're
impeding our Young Persons' Fast Lane.'

'It's a Christmas present from head office.
Actually, it's a bean bag.'

John Jensen